Shakespeare
man of the theatre

illustrated by
Gordon King/Linda Rogers Associates

Macdonald Educational

Growing up in Stratford

Nearly 400 years ago, William Shakespeare wrote and acted in plays that delighted theatregoers of the 16th and early 17th centuries. Today the same plays are being performed all over the world. The stories he created for the stage continue to enchant and capture the imagination of people of all ages, in all countries.

During his own life-time, Shakespeare was known to people in England. But today he is possibly the most famous and celebrated writer in the world. He is best known as a writer of plays (a 'playwright') and as a poet. But he was also an actor, a producer, and eventually a theatre-owner and manager. We know a lot about the theatre at the time he lived. But we know very little about Shakespeare himself. No diaries or letters written by him have survived for us to read now. To this day people are still following up clues, to find out details about his life, just as in a detective story.

We do know that Shakespeare grew up in the busy market town of Stratford-on-Avon, during the reign of Queen Elizabeth I. We know this, because there are written records about Stratford and about Shakespeare's father, who was a well-known citizen and became the town's Mayor for a while. But we really know surprisingly little else about the childhood of the man who became England's most famous playwright. We have to make guesses, from what we know of life in England then.

At that time Queen Elizabeth often travelled round the country visiting different nobles in their great castles and country homes. Many people from her Court travelled with her, and vast, colourful processions took place, which were called 'royal progresses'. Sightseers from all over the surrounding countryside would travel to see them and enjoy the extravagant glittering entertainment provided for the Queen and her following of richly-dressed courtiers.

When Shakespeare was about 11, in the year 1575, the Queen visited the Earl of Leicester at Kenilworth Castle, not far from Stratford.

Isn't it likely that the young boy, Shakespeare, was among the curious visitors from Stratford who hurried to catch a glimpse of the exotic entertainments? Could this have been the boy's first sight of the great Queen whose love of theatrical performances of every kind would play such an important part in his future life?

Players come to Stratford

The people who lived during the reign of Queen Elizabeth (who are usually called 'Elizabethans') were great lovers of music, dancing, and all kinds of entertainment. Among country people in particular, the changing seasons of the year and religious holidays provided many excuses for feasting and celebrations in the villages and towns. May Day and Midsummer Day, the end of a successful harvest, the farewell to the old year and the welcome to the new year—all these occasions had their jubilant festivals.

Stratford nestled then in a wooded valley surrounded by rich farming land. The citizens of this wealthy market town were always ready to welcome wandering groups of actors and comedians.

As a child Shakespeare would frequently have watched tumblers, jugglers and other entertainers performing gaily in the market square.

On May Day, together with other young Stratford people he would have danced round the maypole to welcome spring and the growing season for the crops, and to celebrate the welcome approach of summer warmth.

Stratford was visited regularly by travelling bands of actors. Some on foot and others on horseback, they would have journeyed the dusty, rutted road with their costumes and musical instruments trundling along in a wagon behind. All the tradesmen of Stratford, the cobblers, blacksmiths and bakers, the women and children, would flock excitedly to greet the actors as they entered the town. Then the Mayor would welcome them, and arrange for them to give their first performance in the town hall. After that there would be more performances in the inn on a stage in the open courtyard.

We do not know when Shakespeare first felt the desire to become an actor. Perhaps it was through events like this that he breathed the excitement of the theatre and longed to become part of it.

When he was 18, he married. But these years in his life are still very much a mystery. Even more of a mystery is why—not many years later—he decided to leave his wife and three little children in Stratford, and set out alone on the long dusty road to the great capital, London.

Actors in Stratford. The dragon, defeated by St George, is carried through the town.

To London

London was a bustling hive of a city, stretching along the banks of the great River Thames. The river formed the city's highway and teemed with barges, huge flatboats loaded with goods, and tall-masted merchant ships bound for foreign ports. The only bridge across the Thames was London Bridge. It looked more like a street built out across the water—for it overflowed with houses and shops, and with pedlars and customers struggling from shore to shore with their goods. People also crossed the river by boat-taxi. The air rang with the boatmen crying 'westward ho' and 'eastward ho' to their passengers.

The ancient City, guarded with its walls and gates, and crowned with the steeples of a hundred churches, was London's heart. St Paul's Cathedral, rising high on Ludgate Hill, was its market place. Here crowds of businessmen and lawyers, pedlars and beggars mingled from dawn till dusk. Outside the city walls clustered other places Shakespeare would have known well—the Inns of Court, home of London's law-students, and the theatres rising in the fields on the outskirts of the great capital.

St Paul's Cathedral—the chief meeting place of Elizabethan London.

The Inns of Court— where London's law students lived and studied.

The playhouse in the fields on the edge of London.

Shakespeare joins the theatre

We know that one part Shakespeare played in later years was the 'Ghost' in his own play *Hamlet*.

In London the mystery of Shakespeare's early life continues. He began work in the theatre. This we know because in 1592, about five years after his arrival in the capital, he appears as a well-known and very popular playwright, and as a member of the best acting company of the time.

But what kind of hard work and determination brought him there? At first he probably joined one of the acting companies as a junior actor, or a 'hired man'. He would have been paid about six shillings a week for acting many different small parts—not much, even in those days.

In this way Shakespeare learned all the skills an actor needed. He developed a good strong voice to speak his lines above the noise of the audience (who often chattered ate and drank through the less dramatic parts of a play!) He also had to have a very good memory so that he did not forget his lines—and as he played different parts each afternoon, there was a lot to remember!

An Elizabethan actor had to dance and sing well, to be agile and light-footed and to be a very good swordsman. Battles and sieges, as well as duels and murders, were very popular with the theatregoers. An actor had to learn to fight as if he was really duelling to the death! He had to know how to fall violently without hurting himself or tearing his costume.

At some time in these early years in London, Shakespeare also started to work as a hired writer. First he would have been asked to finish plays begun by other writers, or to brighten up old plays by adding new sections.

But the players' companies badly needed new plays to attract London's audiences. Shakespeare was learning more and more about the theatre. He understood now what the audiences enjoyed and how to construct an exciting, dramatic story for the stage. His talent and imagination were developing fast. In time he was given the chance to write his own plays for the company to perform. And so he began his path to fame in the theatre.

Shakespeare at Elizabeth's Court

The Court of Queen Elizabeth I was then the most
magnificent in Europe. All the great nobles of wealth,
privilege and power gathered round the Queen to form a
Court of great elegance and high fashion. The courtiers,
and particularly the Queen herself, loved entertainment,
singing, music and dancing. They particularly loved
drama, for it could include both poetry and music and
created a world of imagination that every member of the
audience could share. Theatrical performances at Court
usually took place around Christmas. First, Elizabeth's
Master of Revels, who was the man in charge of all Court
entertainment, arranged to have many plays performed
for him by the different companies. He could then choose
one suitable for the Queen and the occasion. It was not
long before the company Shakespeare belonged to was
performing frequently before Queen Elizabeth.

In the Great Hall of one of her many palaces, the Queen
would sit enthroned in the centre of her courtiers,
splendid in her jewels and rich clothes, her red hair
gleaming. A visitor to the Court once described the
performance of Shakespeare's play *Twelfth Night*, when
all the courtiers dressed in white clothes decked with
dazzling gold and brilliant jewels. The picture above
shows Shakespeare's play *A Midsummer Night's Dream*
being performed before the Queen during the wedding
celebrations of the Earl of Derby and his bride.

Performing at Court was a great honour for the players.
It also meant much hard work, for there were many extra
rehearsals and preparations. The Queen knew a great
deal about the theatre, and her standards were very high!
She liked all kinds of plays—comedies for their humour
and gaiety, tragedies for their violence and swift action.

In the public theatre

Acting at Court brought the players valuable approval and fame. But it was the varied, teeming population of London that provided actors and writers like Shakespeare with their main audience. They earned their real living in the public theatres, and won their fame among the citizens of London.

Performances in public theatres took place each afternoon at 2 o'clock. A flag flown high above the theatre announced the forthcoming play and caused the audience to gather in their hundreds. Londoners flocked across the surrounding fields to the theatres—men and women of all classes and all ages. There were the merchants and tradesmen of the City, the lively, noisy crowds of young apprentices (young boys who were learning a trade) and the students from the Inns of Court, the fine ladies and gentlemen of fashion and the elegant young dandies hoping to parade their finery before an admiring audience. And there were the wealthy noblemen, and their many followers.

Performances were lively, noisy, gay affairs. The audience took part energetically, clapping, booing and hissing loudly as the story unfolded on the stage before their eyes. There was much chattering, gambling and flirting before the play began. Booksellers' boys wandered in the galleries, selling the latest books. Sellers of food and drink, their baskets laden with apples, oranges, nuts and ale, pushed to and fro through the jostling crowds throughout the performances.

In the Elizabethan theatre, the stage was in the open air, built so that the audience surrounded it on three sides. Wealthier people bought seats in one of the three high roofed galleries that looked down over the stage and the open yard. Close to the stage, on both sides of it, there were boxes for wealthy noblemen to rent. The young dandies who wanted to display their elegant clothes and figures could rent stools at a high price and sit on the front edge of the stage itself!

For just one penny, everyone else bought room to stand in the open yard. These people were known as the 'groundlings'.

At 2 o'clock, three trumpet blasts pierced the noise and chatter. As the third blast died away, the first player entered, wearing a traditional long black cloak. The audience began to settle down. The afternoon's play had begun at last.

Patrons for the theatre

Although the theatre was popular with many Elizabethans, both rich and poor, there were other people who thoroughly disapproved of it. Some religious preachers thought the theatre and actors were sinful, and that people should stay away from them. Magistrates and city officials did not like large numbers of people collecting in the theatres, because they were afraid of disturbances and riots. They were also afraid that diseases like the Plague might spread very quickly when so many people were so close together.

A law was passed which said that players' companies had to be protected by a nobleman if they wished to perform in public. This protection from a nobleman was like having an official licence to perform plays in public. The nobleman, known as the company's 'patron', provided the players with the 'livery' (or uniform) of his household, and with his badge or coat-of-arms. He and his followers and friends filled the comfortable seats in the playhouse. The players' companies took on the name of their patron.

Shakespeare's company.
At first Shakespeare's company was called Strange's Men after their patron, Lord Strange. But when he died, the company obtained the patronage of the Lord Chamberlain, Lord Hunsdon. They called themselves the Chamberlain's Men and became the Queen's favourite players at Court.

A powerful friend.
The Earl of Essex was the Queen's favourite at Court. He had become famous as a successful and daring commander in naval battles with Spain, and was an ambitious, clever and powerful man.

The Earl of Southampton, Shakespeare's personal patron, was a close friend and follower of Essex. Shakespeare's friendship with these two noblemen greatly affected many of the poems and plays he wrote.

Patrons for poets

Patrons for poets.
Actors' companies had to find patrons so as to be allowed to go on working. But it was also the custom in Elizabethan times for a poet to present or 'dedicate' his work to a nobleman. In return he hoped that the nobleman would offer a generous prize and perhaps offer to become the poet's permanent patron.

Shakespeare's personal patron.
The Earl of Southampton was Shakespeare's patron. He was an elegant, powerful and wealthy young nobleman who was well-liked by the Queen.

We know he was Shakespeare's patron only because Shakespeare dedicated two poems to him. Apart from this, mystery surrounds their friendship, just as it surrounds many details of Shakespeare's private life. We can only make guesses.

The Elizabethan stage

Above: A temporary stage set up in a market place. It was usually a small platform mounted on trestles or barrels. At the back was a cloth-covered booth, usually open at the top, which was used as a dressing room by the actors.

Below: A stage in an inn yard. This was the same kind of stage as above. The audience could watch the play either from the yard, or from the galleries that ran round the inside of the inn.

Elizabethan theatres were very different from those we have now. They were the first permanent theatre buildings. Before they were built, plays were performed on stages specially set up in market places, inn yards or the main rooms of castles, country houses and town halls. The stage in the permanent theatres developed from the style of these original street theatres.

The stage was raised above ground level, and could be viewed by the audience from both sides as well as from the front. In the floor of the stage there was always a trapdoor. It led down to the area below the stage, which was called the 'Hell'. Curtains draped the front of the stage, to hide the 'Hell' from the audience, and actors used the trapdoor and 'Hell' when they played parts such as ghosts rising from the grave, devils leaping from the ground—or whatever else was needed!

At the back of the stage, a wall with doors or curtained doorways on each side hid the actors' dressing rooms and storage areas for costumes and equipment. The actors could wait just behind these doorways, out of sight of the audience, until it was their turn to come on stage. The whole area behind the stage was called the 'tiring house', because it was here that the actors 'attired' (dressed) themselves in their costumes. At the centre of the wall, between the stage doors, there was a small 'inner stage' which could be hidden by curtains. If there was a scene, for example, inside a shop or a cave, these curtains could be pulled back and the inner stage used for the scene.

Above the level of the main stage there was a balcony, or 'gallery'. It was used by musicians sometimes or by actors as a 'mountain top', the 'battlements of a castle', or the 'balcony of a house', according to the play.

Over the stage was a roof, its ceiling painted blue and brightly decorated with golden stars, sun and moon and with exotic figures. This was called the 'Heavens'. Through a trap door in the 'Heavens', machinery which was kept in the 'Hut' above, could lower gods on their thrones, drop shooting stars (fireworks attached to wires), help actors to fly across the stage (using wires) or provide thunder, lightning, or whatever dramatic noises and sights were needed.

The Hut

**The Elizabethan stage.
Front view.**

The Heavens

Gallery

Stage
doors

The Hell

Yard

Wardrobe   and storage

Dressing
rooms

**Cross section of the stage.
Side view, showing the tiring house.**

Stage

The tiring house

A rehearsal

Shakespeare at a rehearsal. One person in the company, probably the leading actor, would have been in charge of the rehearsal. He would guide the movements of the actors and the pace of the play. There was probably also someone who was good at staging a sword fight or putting on a brilliant magical spectacle. He would have had the job of helping the other actors to rehearse these scenes.

In between the public performances each afternoon, the players were hard at work rehearsing and preparing for the next play. And at the same time as Shakespeare was learning parts, rehearsing and acting, he was also writing some of his most popular and successful plays. His day would have been a very full one!

We can imagine what a rehearsal might have been like —a very busy noisy affair! On stage perhaps, one or two actors would rehearse a scene. In the yard, others practised a sword fight or part of a battle. Meanwhile assistants would check the trap-doors and machinery.

The play was always written out and copied by hand. Because of this, very few copies could be made. Only the playwright, the leading actor and the person who reminded actors when they forgot their lines—the 'prompter'—had complete copies. The other actors had only their small part of the play written out for them. But there was always a notice board put up in the theatre with a description of the story, the different scenes and the names of the characters pasted on it. This 'plot', as it was called, gave the company all their instructions, about when to speak, when to go on and come off the stage.

The Plague closes the theatres

Closing the theatres.

Shakespeare with his patron.

The fortunes of the actors' companies were frequently at the mercy of that terrible disease, the Plague. It was carried by rats' fleas from the ships, docks and river-mouths, and thrived on the dirt, crowds and bad air of the city. From victim to victim it crept on, bringing burning fever, pain, horrible suffering and death. At one time it killed over 1000 people a week, and before it ended it had carried off a tenth of London's population. The bodies of the dead had to be buried as quickly as possible, for fear of further disease.

The picture above shows corpses being loaded and carried off in carts through dark deserted streets. It must have seemed as though London itself was dying.

Whenever there was an outbreak of the Plague, all the public meeting places were closed, including the theatres. The City officials hoped that, if people were stopped from gathering together in large numbers, they could prevent the disease from spreading further. But really, only by leaving London did anyone have a chance of escaping the disease.

22

Players on tour. Most travelled on foot. Only the chief actors could afford horses.

With the theatres closed, the actors' companies suffered great hardship. They had to leave London and tour the country in the hope of finding audiences. Travelling was expensive, and audiences in the provinces were much smaller than in London. In some towns people were afraid the actors were bringing the Plague with them, so they were unwilling to watch their plays. All this meant that the actors earned far less money. Often the wages of the 'hired men' had to be cut by half. During one very bad year, 1593, the theatres were closed altogether. Many companies were ruined. Actors had to sell their costumes to get the money to travel back to London. Others were stranded in the country and had to look for other work, so that they could earn money to feed their families.

We don't know where Shakespeare was during the Plague years. There is no evidence that he went on tour with his company. Perhaps he returned to Stratford. Or perhaps for a short time he was a guest of his patron, the Earl of Southampton, who, like other rich people, may have gone to his country home.

New companies, new theatres

After two years, the Plague was over. By the spring of 1594, theatres were allowed to open again. But many of the old acting companies had been ruined. Now the players formed new ones, and looked for new patrons.

Two important players' companies were founded at this time. One was the Chamberlain's Men, with Shakespeare as a member. Shakespeare remained with the Chamberlain's Men for the rest of his career. For them he wrote his best work. The other company was called the Lord Admiral's Men.

Shakespeare was now a 'sharer' in the Chamberlain's Men. This meant that he received a share of the company's earnings. Three men controlled the new company—the chief actor, Richard Burbage, the clown, William Kempe, and Shakespeare himself. The company went from strength to strength, in particular becoming most popular at Elizabeth's Court. But their rivals, the Lord Admiral's Men, also prospered. And there was competition from two other companies, recently formed from young choir boys—one called St Paul's Children (the Choirboys of the Cathedral), and the other the Children of the Chapel Royal. Over the years there was quite a battle for popularity between the different groups.

At first Shakespeare's company used a playhouse called simply the 'Theatre'. It was the first Elizabethan theatre, built in 1576 by James Burbage (the father of Richard Burbage, the chief actor in the Chamberlain's Men). But James Burbage did not own the land on which the Theatre stood, and in about 1598, the man who did began to make difficulties about the Theatre staying there. By now James Burbage was dead.

His sons, Richard and Cuthbert believed that they owned the theatre building and had a right to remove it from the land. So, they organised a group of armed men, headed by a carpenter, and they tore down the Theatre. Then they rowed across the Thames. Before long, an impressive new playhouse was rising above the marshes on the river's southern bank. It was named the 'Globe'. It is this theatre that is best remembered in the story of Shakespeare's life. Here the Chamberlain's Men played for many years.

The Burbages owned half the Globe. Shakespeare and four other players each owned a tenth share. Years later, the thatched roof caught fire during a performance and the building burned down. But before long another Globe theatre rose from the same site.

Shakespeare took a very active part in the design and building of the Globe. After all the years of acting in older buildings he had many ideas about how the new theatre should be planned.

The Globe rose impressively on the south bank of the Thames.

Famous Elizabethan players

There were two actors who were particularly famous on the Elizabethan stage. They were also great rivals. One was the leading actor and joint owner in Shakespeare's company—the great Richard Burbage. The other was the leading actor and founder of the rival company, the Lord Admiral's Men. His name was Edward Alleyn.

Both Richard Burbage and Edward Alleyn played the serious leading parts. But each acted in a very different way. There are descriptions of how Alleyn often strode about the stage, speaking his lines in a thunderous voice, using wide dramatic movements of his arms and hands. Burbage, however, acted in a much quicker and lighter style.

One of the most famous comedians on the Elizabethan stage had also belonged to the Chamberlain's Men. His name was William Kempe. He was well-known and liked not only for his humour but also for the jigs he danced and for his songs. He joined the Chamberlain's Men when they formed in 1594.

Richard Burbage, the leading actor of the Chamberlain's Men. This picture was painted when Burbage was still alive. Some people believe he painted it himself.

Burbage was born into the theatre. His father was James Burbage, the actor who built the first playhouse, the Theatre.

Five years later, in 1599, he was among the joint owners of the new Globe Theatre. But soon afterwards he sold his share and left the company. Their next comedian was named Robert Armin, and he too became very popular.

Shakespeare wrote many of his most famous roles specially to suit the talents of these particular actors. For example he wrote the tragic roles and the leading parts in his plays about English history for Richard Burbage. He wrote the famous 'clown' parts for Kempe and, later, Armin.

The Elizabethan company of players was divided into three main groups. Firstly there were the senior actors such as Shakespeare, Burbage, Kempe and Armin. Secondly there were the 'hired men' who played the smaller parts, as Shakespeare had done when he first joined the theatre. Thirdly there were the boy actors. And they were very important.

In the Elizabethan theatre, there were no women actors. Girls' and young women's parts were always played by boys. Older women were often played by the comedians. Many boys continued to work in the theatre as they grew up, and in time themselves became senior actors. There was always fierce competition between the different boy actors, as well as between the boys and older actors. An actor who had been in the theatre since he was a boy had much more experience than someone like Shakespeare.

The senior actors used to take the boy actors into their homes as pupils. They were given a very strict training, for they had to know how to speak, walk, dance and sing both as a boy and as a girl. Often they had to act both in the same play!

This is a painting of Edward Alleyn, the leading actor and founder of the Lord Admiral's Men. The picture was painted during his lifetime.

Even before Shakespeare left Stratford to go to London, Alleyn was already acting as a member of the Earl of Worcester's company. He was famous for his acting in the plays of another famous playwright of the time, named Christopher Marlowe.

Shakespeare's plays

Shakespeare wrote his plays to suit the kind of audience that would be watching them. Often he wrote plays specially for an important and gay occasion.

So for example, he might write one play for a wedding celebration, or another to be performed during the Christmas season at Court. Others may have been written to please the friends who gathered at the home of his patron, the Earl of Southampton.

Plays written for this kind of occasion were witty and light-hearted. They were designed to amuse, to enchant the eye, to delight the imagination. Very often they were stories of love, of people playing jokes on one another, of people mistaking each other for different people until at last the truth is happily revealed. They were stories of mystery, surprises, discovery and joyful endings.

The Taming of the Shrew
The main characters in this play are Katherina (the Shrew), the hot-tempered eldest daughter of a citizen of Padua, and Petruchio, who has decided to marry her.

This scene shows Katherina and Petruchio's first meeting. Katherina challenges Petruchio to prove he is a gentleman, by hitting him and then daring him to hit her back!

Twelfth Night is the story of a girl, Viola, who is shipwrecked on a lonely coast. She believes that her brother Sebastian, and everyone else on the ship has been drowned. In order to get work at the court of a local Duke, Orsino, she dresses up as a boy page. Her disguise leads to many adventures. But eventually her brother, Sebastian, arrives. He was not drowned after all. This confuses everyone. No one understands that there are now two people who look very alike, both dressed as boys.

The scene shown above tells how the servants of a young widow named Olivia play a trick on her chief servant, a man called Malvolio. They persuade him that Olivia is in love with him. He believes them and so behaves very strangely and very foolishly in front of his mistress. Olivia is horrified, and believing he is dangerously mad, she throws him into prison. He is let out at the end of the play when Olivia discovers the trick the servants have played on him.

The Tempest
This play tells the story of Prospero, the Duke of Milan, who has been exiled by his wicked brother, and put to sea in a rotten boat with his baby daughter, Miranda. They reach an island inhabited only by a half-human creature, called Caliban, and a spirit, Ariel, who become Prospero's servants.

Prospero is a magician and after twelve years uses magic to wreck a ship that is carrying the King of Naples and Prospero's brother. He plans to bring them to the island so he can punish them. In the scene shown here, the spirit Ariel tells Prospero how he wrecked the ship. Behind them, Miranda is asleep.

As You Like It
This scene shows an exiled Duke who is living with his followers in the Forest of Arden. His brother, like Prospero's, has stolen his property and title.

The play tells the story of a young man, Orlando, who falls in love with Rosalind, the daughter of the exiled Duke. Many adventures happen when Rosalind dresses up as a boy, and confuses Orlando, who does not suspect she is really the girl he loves!

Shakespeare's plays: histories

Richard II
This play deals with events between the years 1397 and 1400 during the reign of Richard II. Having exiled his cousin, Henry Bolingbroke, Richard seizes Bolingbroke's land. But Bolingbroke returns and gathers an army to fight Richard. Eventually, in this scene, Richard gives up the crown of England to Bolingbroke, who becomes King Henry IV.

Henry IV Part I
The King's son, Henry Prince of Wales, is a close friend of Sir John Falstaff, a fat jolly rogue, who drinks, eats and boasts a lot.

The Elizabethans very much enjoyed plays about the history of England. Shakespeare wrote a number of plays about different periods in England's history. These plays were designed to interest people like the Earl of Southampton and the Earl of Essex, who were most interested in events at Court, and were soldiers themselves, so they enjoyed plays about the adventures of past kings. The historical plays Shakespeare wrote were *King John*, *Richard II*, *Henry IV*, *Henry V*, *Henry VI*, *Richard III* and *Henry VIII*.

The Prince of Wales and Falstaff act a mock interview between the Prince and his father, the King, who disapproves of the Prince's friendship with someone like Falstaff.

Henry V
King Henry V sets out on a campaign to seize the crown of France. Henry is victorious against the French, and finally marries the French King's daughter. This scene shows Henry preparing to capture the French port of Harfleur.

Richard III
This play describes Richard's climb to the throne of England, murdering many people on the way. Henry Tudor prepares an army to fight Richard. In this scene, the night before the battle, the ghosts of all the people he has killed rise up before him and warn him he will lose the battle. In the battle Richard is killed by Henry Tudor, who becomes King Henry VII.

The fall of Essex

Essex, Southampton and their armed supporters, are halted as they try to leave the city, where Essex had hoped to rally his supporters.

In 1601 dramatic events took place that tragically affected the future of Shakespeare's patron, the Earl of Southampton, and ended in the death of his friend, the Earl of Essex.

   The Earl of Essex had been the Queen's favourite for many years. But recently their relationship had become strained. They had several bad quarrels. Although the Earl of Essex wished to remain in the Queen's favour, there were many people at Court who wanted to disgrace him so that Elizabeth would no longer support him.

In 1599, Essex took on the task of defeating a rebellion in Ireland. He set off with great celebration, certain of his victory, because he was already famous as a soldier. But this time Essex failed. He did not defeat the rebellion. Instead he signed a truce with the rebel leader, Tyrone. Elizabeth was very disappointed and angry with him. She dismissed Essex from Court in disgrace. And so Essex retired sulkily to his London house, a very angry, sad and resentful man. As the months went by, his house became a meeting place for many others who were discontented with the powerful people at Court, who had a lot of influence with the Queen.

Essex became convinced that these people at Court were even plotting to kill him. He decided to gather together his supporters and try to reach the palace at Whitehall and talk to the Queen in person.

But the government soon learned of Essex's plans, and he was proclaimed a traitor. Soldiers were sent to stop Essex. There was a fight on Ludgate Hill, the street leading down from one of the gates of the City of London. Essex escaped from this, but later his home was besieged and he and his supporters were caught, including Southampton. Essex and Southampton were imprisoned in the Tower of London. Essex was found guilty of treason and condemned to death. On a cold February morning in 1601, he mounted the scaffold, splendidly dressed in black satin and velvet. The picture below shows him standing before the executioner.

Southampton was not executed. He was sentenced to life imprisonment, whilst Elizabeth lived, and this was the end of the power and influence of Shakespeare's friend and patron.

Shakespeare's plays: tragedies

Left: **Macbeth**
This is the story of a Scottish general, Macbeth, who is persuaded by his wife Lady Macbeth, to murder the King of Scotland, in order to become king himself. In this scene, Macbeth and another general, Banquo, meet three witches who warn Macbeth that he is to become king, but that Banquo will be the father of future kings. Remembering the witches' promise to Banquo, Macbeth plots to kill him and his son.

Below: **Othello**
The Moor, Othello, is persuaded that his wife, Desdemona, is being unfaithful to him. Finally he kills her, and then learning she was innocent, kills himself.

Shakespeare also wrote plays called the 'tragedies'. These plays are among his most famous works and most often performed today. Some people think that the execution of Essex and the disgrace of Southampton, and all the gloomy events and atmosphere of the last years of Queen Elizabeth's reign, greatly affected Shakespeare, and suggested to him the themes and characters for some of his tragedies.

Here are scenes from some of these tragedies.

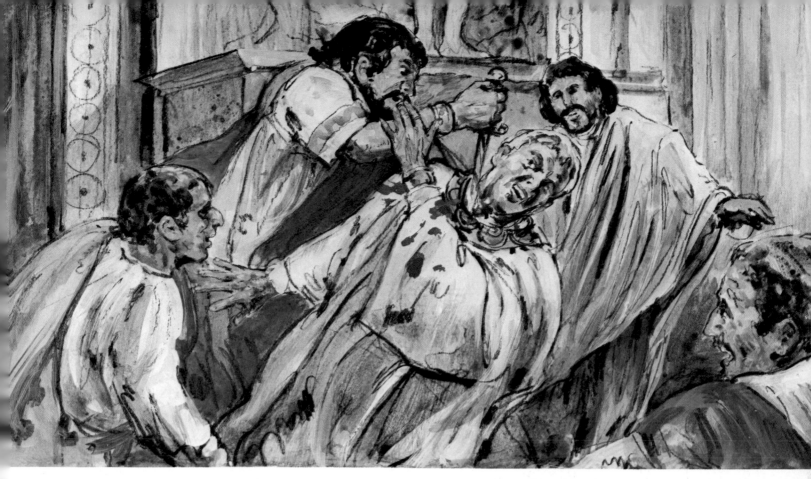

Above: Julius Caesar
This play tells of the murder of
Julius Caesar, and the events which
follow his death as there is a
struggle over who should now rule
in his place. In this scene,
Julius Caesar is stabbed to death.

Below: King Lear
This play tells the story of Lear,
King of Britain, and of the rivalry
between his two wicked daughters,
Goneril and Regan, who wish to get
rid of their father. Only one daughter,
Cordelia, is faithful to her father.

In this scene, King Lear has been
driven out onto a wild heath by
Regan and Goneril. Half mad with
sorrow he wanders in the storm.

One of the King's Men

The year 1603 was the beginning of a new period in the fortunes of Shakespeare and the Chamberlain's Men. In March of that year, Elizabeth I died. She had been Queen of England for 45 years. Now, James VI of Scotland became James I of England, uniting the two Kingdoms, England and Scotland, under his rule. At first there were doubts about whether he would support the theatre as Elizabeth had done. But it was soon learned that the new King and his Queen loved the theatre.

Within 15 days of his arrival in London the King had arranged that the Chamberlain's Men should become his own company. He called them the King's Men, and invited the actor-sharers in the company to take part in his Coronation march. They were given fine crimson cloth to make new clothes.

James I's patronage was even more generous than Elizabeth's had been. He watched about five times as many plays each year. About half of these were performed for him by the King's Men. It was during King James' reign that Shakespeare wrote a number of his most famous plays, including the tragedies *Othello*, *Macbeth* and *King Lear*.

The Chamberlain's Men, now called the King's Men, take part in the Coronation march of James I.

By August 1608 the King's Men had two theatres. The second playhouse, known as the Blackfriars Theatre, was quite different from the Globe. It was an indoor candlelit room, suitable for smaller private audiences. The actors began to use more exotic and expensive scenery. Before long this new theatre was even more profitable than the Globe. And from now onwards Shakespeare was writing plays suitable for both the large public audience of the Globe, and the smaller private audiences of Blackfriars.

Rivals and friends

Christopher Marlowe, the brilliant writer who was stabbed to death during a quarrel at the age of 29. He lived from 1564 to 1593.

Marlowe's plays had a strong influence on Shakespeare's early work. They were acted mainly by Edward Alleyn and the Admiral's Men. Three of his most famous plays are: *Tamburlaine, Dr Faustus,* and *The Jew of Malta.*

We know very little about Shakespeare's private life in London during the reign of James I. But we do know who his friends were, and the name of the inn where he used to meet them, to talk and drink and to compete in wit and brilliant conversation. Many of Shakespeare's friends were also his rivals—fellow playwrights in the competitive life of the theatre and the Court.

On the first Friday of every month, a little group of men used to gather at the Mermaid Tavern in the City. We know who these men were, for they, too, were well-known writers. And we are told that Shakespeare would have been amongst them.

One writer, Ben Jonson, was a close friend and important rival of Shakespeare. He had begun his stage career as an actor in 1597, several years later than Shakespeare. For many years Jonson wrote for the Admiral's Men and for the Children of the Chapel. At some time he also wrote for the Chamberlain's Men, and we know that Shakespeare himself acted in at least one of Jonson's plays. Jonson's work was popular and successful at Court, and by the time he died, some twenty years after Shakespeare, he was considered to be the head of the English literary profession.

The poet, Michael Drayton, who wrote for the Admiral's Men, also joined the gatherings at the Tavern. He seems to have been a very close friend of Jonson and Shakespeare. Another friend was the young poet John Donne, whose daughter Constance was to marry Edward Alleyn, the leading actor of the Admiral's Men.

After 1608, Shakespeare would certainly have met two young writers who were fast becoming successful playwrights—Francis Beaumont and John Fletcher. They wrote many plays together—some specially for the King's Men to perform at the Blackfriars Theatre.

There was one other man who might well have joined that brilliant group at the Tavern, if he had still been alive. His name was Christopher Marlowe. He was a playwright whose plays, when they were first performed, took London's audiences by storm. But tragically, he had died in 1593 at the age of 29, stabbed to death during a quarrel in an inn.

Quieter years in Stratford

By 1611, when Shakespeare was 47, he had worked in the theatre as an actor and a playwright for more than 20 years. He had made a small fortune from the success of the theatre company, and was recognised as a brilliant writer. But now it seems that he was growing tired.

About this time he began to make plans to retire from the theatre and from London. Some years before he had bought a house in Stratford. His family was already living there. Now seemed the right time to join them and begin to lead a more peaceful and relaxed life. So in 1611 he sold his share of the ownership of the two theatres, the Globe and the Blackfriars, and returned to Stratford.

Shakespeare's home in Stratford was called New Place. It was a large, elegant house with two barns, two orchards and a fine flower garden. Stratford people usually called it the Great House. Here Shakespeare spent most of his time from 1611 onwards. But he continued to write for the King's Men, and he did return to London now and again. We know he returned in 1613, for that was a particularly busy time for the King's Men. The King's daughter, Princess Elizabeth was getting married, and eight of Shakespeare's plays were performed at the Court celebrations.

After this he retired once more to Stratford. His life changed completely. He became a country gentleman, surrounded usually in peace and quiet by his family and friends. He had spent so little time with them in all the past years, and now his daughters, Judith and Susanna were grown up. Susanna was married and had a daughter.

Shakespeare also enjoyed entertaining his London friends. Ben Jonson and Michael Drayton visited him in Stratford. According to one story (told by a Stratford vicar), during the spring of 1616, 'Shakespeare, Drayton and Ben Jonson had a merry meeting, and it seems drank too hard, for Shakespeare died of a fever . . .'

In fact, no one really knows what caused Shakespeare's death. All we do know, from the date carved on his tomb in Stratford, is that he died on April 23, 1616. On a flagstone over his tomb are carved these strange words:
'Good friend, for Jesus sake forbear
To dig the dust enclosed here:
Blest be the man that spares these stones,
And curst be he that moves my bones.'

Perhaps it was Shakespeare himself who wrote these final words—leaving behind one last mystery for all lovers and students of Shakespeare.

Famous Shakespearian actors

Thomas Betterton lived from 1635-1710. He was famous for his acting as 'Hamlet'. He was married to Mary Saunderson, the first woman actor to perform in Shakespeare's plays.

Shakespeare himself died. But his plays live on. They are performed in the 20th century as they have been performed in every century since he first left Stratford.

Each century has found new actors on the stage, who have given fresh life and new excitement to the characters Shakespeare created. For millions of theatregoers, they have brought alive again the tragedies and the comedies, with their drama and sorrow, humour and wit, that Shakespeare wrote for those distant audiences of the 16th and 17th centuries.

On this page are drawings or photographs of some of these famous actors. There have been many others who are not mentioned here, only because there isn't enough room to write about them all.

Towards the end of the 17th century, women actors began to appear in Shakespeare's plays, instead of the boy actors who had always played girls' parts during Shakespeare's lifetime.

Many of the actors shown here lived long before photography was invented. But artists drew pictures of the actors when they appeared upon the stage.

Left: **Mrs Siddons**. She lived from 1755 to 1831. She started acting as a child. She first appeared on stage in the play *Macbeth* in the part of Lady Macbeth.

Above: **David Garrick**. He lived from 1717 to 1779. He became very famous for the way he acted the part of Richard in Shakespeare's play *Richard III*.

Above: **Henry Irving,** who lived from 1838-1905, played the parts of *Hamlet, Othello, Richard II* and *Macbeth*. From 1879, he acted and produced many Shakespeare plays with Ellen Terry.

Ellen Terry is shown below. She lived from 1848 to 1928, and first went on the stage when she was eight years old.

Above: **Sarah Bernhardt** was a French actress, who lived from 1834 to 1923. She played some of the leading roles in Shakespeare's plays. One of her first successes was in *King Lear* as the King's loyal daughter, Cordelia.

Right: **Edwin Booth** was an American actor who produced many of Shakespeare's plays. He played most of the main parts. His most famous part was Hamlet. He lived from 1833-1893.

In the 20th century there have been many famous Shakespearian actors, both men and women. **Sir Lawrence Olivier** is one of them. He has played Shakespearian parts both on the stage and in films.

Shakespeare today

These are photographs of Shakespeare's plays performed by the Royal Shakespeare Company.

Above: A scene from the *Merry Wives of Windsor,* performed in 1975.

Below: A scene from *A Midsummer Night's Dream,* performed in 1970. The actors are wearing modern clothes. Compare this with the picture on pages 12-13, which shows the play being performed before Queen Elizabeth.

Ben Jonson said of his friend Shakespeare, 'He was not of an age, but for all time.' Shakespeare does not belong to just one period of time. His work can be enjoyed today as it was by the audiences who first saw it nearly 400 years ago. His plays have often been acted and produced very much as we imagine Shakespeare wanted them to be. But they have also been produced in very different ways, using modern clothes, the costumes of different centuries, and adapting the original play to suit the interests and tastes of a different period or a different country.

Some countries have built special theatres for performing Shakespeare's plays. The first one was built in Stratford, and is called the Royal Shakespeare Theatre. Others have been built in Canada and America. Every year in Stratford, there is a Shakespeare festival. The season of plays lasts for eight months, and attracts audiences from all over the world.

But it is interesting to remember that if it had not been for the efforts of two of Shakespeare's fellow actors, soon after his death, we may never have fully discovered what a great writer he was. Three years after Shakespeare, in 1619, Richard Burbage died. Now only two members of the original Lord Chamberlain's Company were left— John Heminge and Henry Condell. They knew that there was great danger that much of Shakespeare's work would be lost. Very few copies of it had been made, though a great deal remained in the memories of actors who had worked with him. They decided to gather and preserve as many of the plays as they could. But it was a difficult task. Most of the original manuscripts had been lost. Some of the prompter's copies still remained. In many cases they had to sort through many confused and wrongly-printed copies. They had to use their memories to decide how Shakespeare's language had been changed in the printing. Then they tried to restore his plays, so that they were as Shakespeare originally wrote them. And so in 1623, the first edition of Shakespeare's collected plays was printed. Through this, the work of the great writer was kept for us. Now, as long as there are actors to speak the lines he wrote, Shakespeare will continue to exist.

During the 20th century, the development of film-making has meant that Shakespeare's plays can be performed not only in the theatre but also for cinema and television audiences.

Above: A photograph of a scene from the film *Macbeth*.

Right: A photograph of a scene from the film *Romeo and Juliet.*

Some important names

These are some of the most important names mentioned in this book. You can find them on the pages listed below.

Shakespeare's plays: the following ones are mentioned in this book